IN THE HOURS OF
MEDITATION

F. J. ALEXANDER

Advaita Ashrama
(Publication Department)
5 Dehi Entally Road
Kolkata 700 014

Published by
Swami Mumukshananda
President, Advaita Ashrama
Mayavati, Champawat, Himalayas
from its Publication Department, Kolkata
Email: *mail@advaitaonline.com*
Website: *www.advaitaonline.com*

ISBN 81-7505-047-0

Printed in India at
Trio Process
Kolkata 700 014

into work and rendered valuable help in bringing out a Life of the Swami Vivekananda, by

PREFACE

The present book, originally published under a modest pseudonym, came from the pen of
F. J. Alexander, whose promising career has been
cut short by the cruel hand of death. His early
years were spent in the nunnery of Omaha in
Nebraska, U.S.A., where he received his first education. But the cloistered atmosphere of an old-
world nunnery became too much for a boy of his
spirits, and he made good his escape to enjoy the
freedom of the wider world. He began life as a
bell-boy at a hotel in an American city, and after
various turns of fortune entered a newspaper of-
fice, where he showed himself as a good and im-
pressive writer. But all along he had been seized
with a great spiritual unrest, which knew no qui-
etude till he came across, by chance some writings
of the Swami Vivekananda, which opened the
vista of a new world before him. The call of his
Master—The Swami Vivekananda was hence-
forth regarded by him as such—was so strong that
he afterwards sailed for India to consecrate himself to the service of the Order founded by him.

3

Mr. Alexander came to the Math at Belur in 1911, and then joined the Advaita Ashrama at Mayavati. Here he threw himself heart and soul into work and rendered invaluable help in bringing out a Life of the Swami Vivekananda, by which his name will be immortalized. He was also an attractive writer—anonymously or under various pseudonyms—to the *Prabuddha Bharata*, from which these pages have been reprinted. From Mayavati he went to Almora to live a more intense spiritual life. After two years of stay there, he went back to America to recuperate his failing health, and there succumbed to tuberculosis in 1917.

Whoever came in contact with him was struck by his vigorous mind and childlike heart, and it is wonderful to see how deeply he was imbued with the Indian spirit and ideals. The following pages, clearly reflecting his inner life, show the depth of his spiritual fervour. May this Disciple's thoughts rising *'in the hours of meditation'* serve as a beaconlight to thousands of kindred spirits struggling for Realization!

THE PUBLISHER

4

IN THE HOURS OF MEDITATION

I

There are hours when one forgets the world. There are hours when one approaches that region of blessedness in which the Soul is Self-contained and in the presence of the Highest. Then is silenced all clamouring of desire; all sound of sense is stilled. Only God IS.

There is no holier sanctuary than a purified mind, a mind concentrated upon God. There is no more sacred place than the region of peace into which the mind enters when it becomes fixed in the Lord. No more sweet-odorous and holy incense is there than the rising of thought unto God.

Purity, bliss, blessedness, peace! Purity, bliss, blessedness, peace! These make up the atmosphere of the state of meditation.

The spiritual consciousness dawns in these silent, sacred hours. The soul is close to its source. The streamlet of personality expands in these hours, becoming a mighty, swiftmoving river, flowing in the direction of that true and permanent individuality which is the Oceanic Consciousness of God. And this is one and only.

In the hours of meditation the soul draws from On High those true qualifications which are of its nature—fearlessness, the sense of reality, the sense of deathlessness.

Draw within thy Self, O Soul! Seek thou the silent hour with truth. Know thou thy Self to be of the substance of truth, the substance of Divinity! Verily within the heart doth God dwell!

II

Fear not! All mortal things are as shadows. Unreality dominates all appearance. Thou art the Reality within which no change abides. Know thou art the Immovable One! Let nature play with thee as nature will. Thy form is a dream. Know this, and be thou content! Thy soul is stationed in the formlessness of Divinity. Let the mind follow the blinking light; desire rules, limitations exist. Thou art not mind; desire touches thee not. Thou art contained within Omniscience and Omnipotence. Remember life is but a play. Play thy part. Thou must. Such is the law. Yet, withal, thou art neither player, play nor law. Life itself cannot limit thee. Art thou not limitless! Life is of the stuff of dreams. Thou dreamest not. Thou art the Dreamless One beyond the touch and taint of unreality. Know this! Know this and be free—free—free!!!

Peace! Peace! Silent, audible Peace! Peace wherein the Voice of God is heard. Peace and Silence! Then comes the Voice of God, audible—audible within the Silence!

'I am with thee, ever and for ever. Never hast thou been nor canst thou be from Me apart. I am

7

thy Soul. Verily thy Soul is I. Beyond the universe, beyond all dreams I rest, Self-contained within immensity. And even so art thou; ay, even so art thou. For I am thou and thou art I. Leave off all dreams! Come! Come unto Me! I shall carry thee across the ocean of darkness and ignorance unto Light and Life Everlasting. For I am these; and thou and I are One. Thou art I! I am thou! Go, dwell in Peace! Dwell thou in Peace! Again when the hour cometh, in the stillness and in the Peace thou shalt hear My Voice!'—the Voice of God—the Voice of God!

III

Again the hour is at hand. Day merges in the evening time. Everywhere without is quiet. Nature herself is at peace. And when nature is at peace, more peacefully does the soul retire into the inner chamber of the heart. More readily also. Let the senses and their activity subside. Life, as it is, is short; desire is rampant. Give at least some short time unto the Lord. He asketh little, only this, that thou shalt know thy Self; for, verily, knowing thy Self, thou comest to know Him. For God and the Soul are One. Some say, 'Remember, O Man, that thou art dust!' True, of the body! Even of the mind is it true! But the higher, the mightier, the truer, the holier revelation reads, 'Remember, O Man, that thou art the Soul!'

'Indestructible and imperishable art thou alone, O Soul!' So speaketh the Lord. All else wanes. However mighty the form, it perishes. Death and destruction are the lot of all form. Thought is subordinate to change. Personality is of the weaving of these—thought and form. Therefore, stand aside, O Soul. Remember thou art the Self beyond both thought and form. All virtue resides in this consciousness, 'Thou art One with God.' In this alone art thou immortal; in this alone art thou pure and holy.

Try not to *become* the master. Thou *art* the master! There is no becoming for thee. Thou *art*, O Soul! However sublime may seem the process of *becoming*, the hour shall come when thou shalt know. 'Progress is in time', but 'Perfection is within eternity.' And thou art not of time. Thou art of eternity.

Is there Divinity! Then, 'Tat Tvam Asi!'—meaning, 'Thou art That! Thou art That!' Understand that which is the Highest within thee. Worship the Highest! And the most perfect form of worship is the knowledge that thou and the Highest are One. And what is the Highest? That, O Soul, thou callest God.

Throw all dreams into oblivion! Having heard of the Self within thee, the Self thou art, understand! Having understood, perceive! Having perceived, know! Having known, realize! Having realized, then—'Tat Tvam Asi!'—which is, 'Thou art That!'

Retreat from the world! It is the embodiment of dreams. It together with the body—verily, these are the nests of dreams. Shalt thou be a dreamer? Shalt thou be bound for ever in the bondage of dreams? 'Arise! Awake! and stop not till the goal is reached!'

So speaketh the Lord in the Silence—in the deep, deep Silence when only His Voice is audible. Hari! Om Tat Sat! 'Go thou in Peace!' Beyond all, ay, even within all appearance of form reigns the Spirit. Its nature is Peace, Peace, Unutterable Peace!

IV

The Voice of God, speaking, saith in the Quiet Hour, 'Remember, ever remember, "Only the pure in heart see God!" Purity is the first requisite. Even as they who are governed by desire are intense therein in their passions, even so be thou pure; even so, do thou have a passionate longing for purity! Search deeply and steadfastly for purity. It alone availeth. Call to thy mind that great prayer of My servant, Prahlada, unto Me, "O Lord, that same intensity of love that worldly people have for the fleeting objects of the senses, give to me that same intensity of love for Thee!" Purity is the antechamber to the Lord's Presence. Before thou thinkest of the Lord, think of purity. Purity is the key by which the doors of meditation that lead into the Abiding-Place of the Most High, are opened.

'Throw thyself upon the Ocean of My Strength. Strive not! Seek not! *Know* that I AM. This knowledge, added with complete resignation unto My Will shall save thee. Have thou no fears! Art thou not in Me! Am I not in thee! Know thou that all this passes which men deem so great. Death is everywhere, swallowing up the forms of life. Death and change ensnare and bind all things—save the Spirit. Know this! Purity is the method of this knowledge. It is the foundation-ground. With purity comes fearlessness, freedom and the realization on thy part of thine own nature, the reality of which I AM.

'Let the tempest blow, but when desire burns and the mind vacillates—then, THEN call upon ME! I shall hear. For, as My servant hath said, I hear even the footfall of an ant. And I shall speed unto thee. I do not desert them who call upon Me sincerely. Call upon Me, not only sincerely, but steadfastly as well.

'I am not the universe; I am the *Spirit* beyond it! The universe is as a carcase unto Me. I am concerned with the SOUL alone. Be not deceived by the external magnitude of things. Divinity is not in form, not yet in thought. It is the purified, free, spiritual, blissful, form-emancipated, thought-emancipated consciousness which knows not, nor can know, any stain or sin or bondage or limitation. Within the innermost, That art thou, O Soul. Realization shall come to thee with regard to this. It must. For such is the Sure Goal of the soul's life. Remember, remember I am with thee! I am with thee! I, the Lord, am with thee! I am as Strength

13

to all thy weakness; I am as Forgiveness to all thy sin; I am as Love to all thy search for Me! I am thy Self! I am thy Self! Put off all other thoughts of Self! For in the thought that thy Self is in any wise different from the Self of Me lies all ignorance and all weakness. Arise, thou Shining One, know that I am thy Self! I am thy Self.

'And purity is the pathway to My Presence! Herein is thy salvation! Hari! Om Tat Sat!

'Peace! Peace! Peace!'

V

The Voice of the Guru, who is God, speaks:
'Lo! I am ever with thee. No matter where thou
goest, I am already there. I live for thee. The fruit
of my realization I bequeath unto thee. Thou art
the treasure of my heart, the apple of mine eye.
We are one in God. Our business is realization. So
well do I realize my oneness with thee—I fear not
to cast thee into the wilderness of the world and
into the forest of doubt. It is because I know the
measure of thy powers. Through experience after experience I sent thee; but always doth my eye
follow thee in thy wandering. Dost thou sin? Thou
sinnest in my presence. Dost thou perform virtu-
ous acts? I perceive them all. I know all thy moods.
Through all manner of experience and of thought
I fasten the bonds that are between us. My salvation is naught to me, unless thou dost take part in
it. Thou art the Self of me in another form. The
more thou dost absorb the vision which is mine,
lo! the more and more do we grow into that spiritual oneness which is the Divine Life. The veils
of separate personality fall off and thou art mine
own Self and mine own Self is thou. So close are

the bonds. Death and separation have no hold in my relationship to thee. For though thou mayest be born far apart and though thou mayest not have even seen the physical form I wore, still none the less art thou my very own. Discipleship does not consist in having seen my form, but in having understood my will. Thou canst never escape the net I have cast out.

'Seek out my will. Follow the teaching which the Master has given unto me and which I have transmitted unto thee. See thou the same vision which is mine. Then shalt thou be more at one-ness with me than hadst thou dwelt near a myriad bodies which were mine. Discipleship consists in steadiness of devotion to my thought and will. And immeasurable love is between us. Go thou in peace. Harder than adamant are the bonds of re-lationship between Guru and disciple. Stronger than death are they. For they are tied by Immea-surable Love and the Divine and Omnipotent Will.

'Om Tat Sat!'

The Disciple responds in praise and thanks-giving:

'Ay, my Lord, my god, my all in all. So am I taught. The Guru is God. He yearns to merge in

16

the Divine Reality. His vision is of God. Untiring is his zeal in the salvation of my soul. Through the eyes of the Guru, I also see the vision. True love is stronger than death; ay, stronger than birth as well is love. Birth and death may separate me from his presence. What do I say? False!! The Guru is God. Can I at any time be separated from God! Taking His Name I shall struggle through this ocean of darkness safe to that other shore where all is wisdom and radiance. I shall march fearlessly through this interminable jungle of illusion, for He is watching all my movements and, if I fall, He shall raise me up. Are there thorns in my path, lo! He will brush them aside. Do the wild animals of doubt and temptation beset me, lo! He will slay them. Or, perhaps, He will let me fall into their path. He will make me struggle with them in order to reveal my own powers to myself. And how shall a man know His powers until he has tested himself?

'Birth and death are nothing to me. I shall tear aside all limitations. I shall go beyond all bonds. I shall see the Divinity in Him. That self-same Reality which is in me, O Guru, is likewise within Thee. Thou art the Sun and I the ray. Even so am I the Sun and Thou the ray. The great utterance of Self-revelation of the Upanishads, "Tat

Tvam Asi—Thou are That", applies to Thee; it applies to me. O the sense of Unutterable Oneness!

    'Adoration to the Guru as Guru! Adoration to the Guru as God.

Om Tat Sat!

Tat Tvam Asi!

Aham Brahmasmi!'

VI

In the hours of meditation the soul speaking to itself sayeth:

'Peace dwelleth in the Silence. And to gain Peace thou must be strong and the silence cometh when the tumult of sense has been drowned in the Powerful Stillness of Renunciation. Thou art a wanderer in the desert of this world. Tarry not lest thou dost perish by the wayside. Make thy caravan of good thoughts and provide thyself with the Waters of a Living Faith. Beware of all mirages. The goal is not *there*. Be thou not deceived by the attraction of externals. Renouncing all, go thou by those paths which lead thee into the solitude of thine own insight. Follow thou not the many caught within the net of manifoldness. Go thou along the paths whereby saints journey singly and separately to the goal of Oneness. *Dare* to be brave. Conquest lies in making the initial effort. Do not waver. *Plunge* into sanctity. With one mad leap drown thyself in the Ocean of God. Divinity is the End. In the nature of things there could be none other for thee—thou shining ray of the Effulgent One!

'Make haste, lest thou repent. Whip up the steeds of religious earnestness and powerful faith. Crush thyself if need be. Let nothing stand in thy path. Thine is no chance destiny. March thou on with surety and strength of soul, for thy destination is Reality. Verily, thou thyself art the Real. Be thou Free! Be thou Free! In all the language of Self-realization none such valuable word is there as Strength. First—last—and always, be thou strong. Fearing neither heavens nor hells, neither gods nor demons, go thou forth! Nothing shall conquer thee. God Himself is bound to *serve* thee; for He is attracted by That which is Himself in thee. And thus Oneness is the Essence of Sublime Insight for That which is *in* thee—That which is thee is God. Verily thou thyself art Divine.

Tat Tvam Asi! Hari Om Tat Sat!

'Dost thou believe! Have faith in thy Self! How canst thou believe in God if thou believest not in thine own Self? Thou must save thyself. "God helps those who help themselves." Take cognizance of thy Real Self; measure It according to the *Spiritual* standard. Know thou art *not* the body. Even thought art thou not. Thought is the method of seeing, but the vision is the end. Thus the final truth is Realization. The final mandate is, "Man, know thy Self"—man, realize thy nature. Faith! Faith! Faith! Everything depends on Faith. Not the Faith which is belief, but the Faith which is Vision. There is no other sin but doubt; learn to hate doubt as thou dost poison; the greatest weakness is doubt. To doubt one's Self—that, indeed, is blasphemy. Be thou afraid of naught—nay, not even of God, for God is to be *loved*, not feared. How canst thou fear thy Self! And God is the Self of thee! There is naught but God! And thou art That! Therefore, "Arise! Awake! and stop not till the goal is reached!" Such is the Gospel of the Blessed One!'

IN THE SILENCES OF MEDITATION

VII

The Soul, speaking further in the times of
meditation, sayeth unto itself:

'True, the hour of trial cometh, and human
weakness is great; but then the very knowledge
that sin is weakness will in time destroy it. For
when once thou knowest poison, naturally thou
wilt abhor it. When thou knowest thy weakness, it
shall no more be weakness. Thou hast laid bare
the heart of thy trouble, and that which is the
Depth in thee will alter the currents of its move-
ment. In time thou shalt conquer—so long as the
heart is sincere. And pray steadfastly, for constant
vigilance of soul is required in the spiritual
struggle. Now and then moments will come when
thou shalt have insight into thy real nature, and
thou shalt know weakness as weakness. In that
time call upon the Lord, and He, heeding thy
prayer, shall give thee Grace.

'Theory is one thing and life another. Realize that no matter how wonderful thy intellectual
awareness of truth may be—man-making is the
goal. Realization is all in all. The beast in thee is
strong; but it can be tamed down by sincere

prayer. Prayer is the one thing. Only prayer can conquer lust. Noting is greater than the name of God. *Constant Vigilance* be thy motto and *Constant Prayer*. And they who are the Helpers, the Messengers of the Most High, shall come and thou shalt be free! Indeed, long is the way, but the end is sure! Prayer goes deep; it eats out the vitals of temptation. Pray, pray—pray constantly, pray always. And be not discouraged in the evil hour; be not discouraged when thou dost fall. God is always near. He knows thy woe and thy sincerity, but never leave off calling upon Him! Even in thy sin be strong in prayer. From out the depth of prayer, all things come—love for God, spiritual vision, and spiritual realization. Take thy stand upon the thought that God is All-Powerful and that His nature is that of the good shepherd who guides his sheep *specially* when they go astray. Know that before God is Author of Justice, He is Love Itself. Do thou but ask and it shall be given unto thee; do thou but seek and thou shalt find; do thou but knock and it shall be opened unto thee. Make but the feeblest effort; even that shall lift thee up into the kingdom of righteousness.

'Ay, every prayer which thou utterest, each rising of thy heart unto God shall be added unto thee, giving thee strength. Thy prayers shall make thee whole. Depend on prayer! It is the means. However dark thy heart, prayer shall bring light therein, for prayer IS meditation; prayer in itself IS vision. Prayer is communion with the Almighty. It links thee with Omnipotence and Supreme Love. It lends wings to thy soul. Even if thou art in the mire, thou shalt rise. Even if mountainloads of iniquity have fallen upon thee and have buried every vestige of thy spirituality, prayer will raise thee up. And from the depths God will hear thee and His Love and Power shall be made manifest unto thee, and thou shalt be lifted up as a testimony of the words of the Most High. And thou shalt sing a song, magnifying God who is thy Saviour. And thine own heart shall testify to the greatness of the Mercy of the Lord; and all who have ever known thee shall say, "Lo! He hath become a saint!" Verily His Mercy is His Justice and His Mercy endureth for ever and ever. Hold on to prayer! No matter how numerous the temptations that assail thee as enemies, by prayer thou shalt build a fortress about thy nature and it shall be impregnable. Ay, even the Gates of Hell shall not prevail against it! For God shall have bound thee unto Him by the strong cords of Love and Realization that come of prayer!'

Hari Om Tat Sat!

VIII

The Voice of the Guru speaks in the inmost silence of the heart:

'My son, the Flesh wars constantly against the Spirit! Therefore be constantly on the alert. How hollow is life! Trust not the senses. These are swayed by pleasure and by pain. Go thou beyond! Thou art the Soul! At any moment the body may go! Indeed, who knows the hour! Therefore keep thy vision fixed unalterably on the Ideal. Saturate thy mind with ennobling thoughts. Not in the hour of death, but in the hours of life keep thy mind free and pure. Then, if death overtake thee of a sudden, thou art prepared. Live thy life as though thou wert even now about to die. Then shalt thou truly live. Time is fleeting, but thou canst make eternity of time provided thou dost think eternal and immortal thoughts.

'When thy body goes down into death, certainly thou shalt repent IF thou hast not lived the life of thy ideals here on earth. Ah! IF—that fatal word which spells neglect and remorse. Thousands are the spirits who lament, saying, "O, IF I had only done so in the body, I would now be nearer to my God!" Therefore throw thy whole soul at this very moment with all the sincerity of thy being into the Ideal. Say, "O God! MAKE me have the Vision of Thee! *Make* me sincere. *Make* me yearn for thee!" Say to thyself every day that great prayer of all the devotees, "Let me love Thee alone, O Lord!"

'The Spirit of Man is infinite. Infinite Power is at thy beck and call. Realize that thou art of the Soul of God. He breathes in thee; He lives in thee; He moves in thee; thou hast thy very being in Him. When this thou dost realize, all fear shall drop off from thee. Thou shalt attain to the state of fearlessness.'

And the soul, in response to the Voice of the Guru says, 'O Lord! Thou Author of all things, Thy nature is Infinite Love! Thou art everywhere. O grant that I be possessed of this consciousness intensely! In all the worlds there is no hope but in Thee! Terror and the forms of death are everywhere. Pain and illusion are on all sides. Such is the vision of mortal life. But do thou remove the illusion! Then, where death stalks and where life is pain I shall behold Thee! O let me behold Thee even in the Terrible. O Thou Destroyer of Illusion, hear my prayer!'

And the Voice of the Guru makes answer:

'My son, call upon the Lord! Call always upon the Lord. Think of Him, and Him alone, and the Power that is Infinite shall surround thee, and the Love that is Infinite shall embrace thee, and He shall speak words of realization to thy soul. True dependence upon god solves all difficulties. The process of true Man-making is in complete resignation to the Supreme Love; it is manifest in uninterrupted meditation. When life is seen as fraud, when death is present, when the heart is wrung with agony, and human woe attains its climax—remember, make thou the effort to remember, that these things are of the body and that thou art the Soul. Take hold of each day as if it were thy last. Make Japa of it every moment of thy life. Daily consecrate thy life to God. See the Wisdom of His Will. And then, even in the mouth of a tiger, even in the presence of death, even on the threshold of hell, thou shalt find God.

'If this be thy life's labour—to remember God—then a great joy and a serene peace shall abide with thee, and that which seems gruesome shall become beautiful, and that which seems terrible shall become all-loving. And with the saint, bitten by a cobra, thou shalt joyfully exclaim. "Behold! Behold! A Messenger has come from my Beloved", or with the saint, in the tiger's mouth, thou

27

shalt call out "Shivoham! Shivoham!" And this is the Strength of the Soul. This is verily Its manifestation. This is the Spirit of the Divine—because it is the Perception of the Divine.

'The warrior rushes to the cannon's mouth in defence of the motherland. The mother rushes into fire and into water and into the tiger's mouth to save her child. The friend dies for the sake of his friend. The Sannyasin bears all hardships for the sake of the Ideal. Do thou bear all trials, face all dangers, live the Life of Ideals, and be brave and fearless IN THE NAME OF GOD. Thou art my son. In death or in life, in sin or in virtue, in pleasure or in pain, in good or in evil, whithersoever thou goest, wheresoever thou art, I am with thee, I protect thee, I love thee. For I am bound to thee. My love for *God* makes me one with *thee*. I protect thee! I love thee! I am thy very Self. Child, thy heart is My abode!'

Hari Om Tat Sat!

IX

There came a Voice resonant with Divinity. It said, 'Oh, there is a Love which fears nothing, which is greater than life and greater than death. I am that Love. There is a Love which knows no limit, which is everywhere, which is in the presence of death, and which is all-Tender even in the Terrible. I am that Love. There is a Love which is Unutterably Sweet, which welcomes all pain, which welcomes all fear, which drives away all sadness, which is wheresoever thou dost search for it. I am that Love. Oh, I am the very Essence of that Love. And, O, My own Self, I, that Love, am Thine own Self, My nature is Love! I *am* Love Itself!

'Oh, there is a Beauty which is all-comprehending. It knows neither ugliness nor shortcomings. It is sublime. It is divine. Oh, there is no limit to this Beauty! It is like the expanse of the sky or the depth of the seas. It is manifest in odorous dawns and in flaming sunsets. It is manifest in the roar of a tiger and the song of a bird. It is manifest as storm and as peace, but is *beyond* these. These are its aspects. I am that Beauty. There is a

29

Beauty which is much deeper than pleasure and much deeper than pain. This is the Beauty of the Soul. I am that Beauty! Oh, I am that Beauty! Of all attraction, whatever its character, I am the Centre, I am the Magnet; all other things are iron filings, some drawn this way, some that, but all are drawn—irresistibly. Oh, I am that Magnet! I am that Beauty! I am that Attraction, and My Nature is Blessedness.

'Oh, there is a Life which is Love, which is Blessedness! I am that Life! Nothing circumscribes that Life; nothing can limit it; and this is the Life Infinite. It is Eternal Life, and I am that Life. Its Nature is Peace, and I am Peace. Within its all-embracingness there is no strife, no hurried coming and going, no ruthless attempt to live, no desire to procreate. IT IS. I am that Life. Neither the stars nor the sun can contain It. It is a Light which no other Light can outshine. It is Itself Light. There is no gauging the depths of this Life. There is no measuring Its Heights. I am that Life. And thou art in Me and I am in Thee.

'Unsustained, sustaining everything, I am the Spirit in all forms that are. I am the Silence within the Sound of Life. I am Eternity woven on the warp and woof of Time. I am the Self beyond both form and thought. Mindless, yet am I omniscient. Formless, yet am I everywhere. Containing naught, I am contained in everything. I am Power! I am Peace! I am Infinity! I am Eternity! I am the Unifying Unit of all Plurality. I am the Sum and Substance of all living things. Of all warring parts I am the whole! Beyond the spheres of life and death I dwell deathless, birthless, beyond bondage. Who finds Me out, he is the Free, the Free!

'Through all illusion I perceive Reality. I am Reality perceived! I am the Wielder of this magic force, this Shakti, this Maya which is the Mother's Form. From out the Womb of Time I take My birth, embodying Myself in All that is of Form. I *am* the Womb of Time, and thus Eternity. And "Thou art That," O Soul, which is in ME, the Self. Therefore, arise, awake, and tear all bonds to shreds. Wipe out all dreams, dispel illusion's hold. Thou art the Self! The Self art thou! Naught can hinder thee from the realization of thy nature. Arise! Arise! Stop not until the Goal is reached— the Goal which is the Self, the Life, the Love, the Bliss Eternal and the Knowledge of the soul made Free!'

X

And the Voice of the Guru spoke unto my soul:

'Man, where is thy Faith! Art thou a beast that thou goest quaking at every danger! Until thou hast overcome the body idea, thou canst not realize the Truth! Art thou then a carcase! Wilt thou for ever dance in that mire of physical dirt! Come out of thy smallness! Come forth! Be a man! Where is thy Divinity if it remains for ever unexpressed! Art thou then so important that the world stands in need of thee! Overcome the self by the Self. Be Free! If thou strivest after the Imperishable death shall not touch thee, for thou shalt have lost the knowledge of what death is. Thine shall be Immortality. All the world has been struggling to express Reality—but the very first success in this effort is the spelling of character. Character is everything. Make character! Make character! Every hour do thou make character! Dwell thou in thy spirit upon the Deathless, and thou shalt become deathless! Make thine abode Reality—and then neither birth nor death, nor the varying experiences of life shall cause thee fear.

'Let the body go! Give up clinging to it! Free thyself in mind! The whole meaning of religion and of ethics is to overcome the animal consciousness, confined in sex and fear and sleep and food. Give it up! Give up this clinging to the carcase! Call it the carcase! Regard it as such at all times. Throw no gold cloth over it. It is filth. Only the Spirit is real. The consciousness of the Spirit is immortality. The thinking of immortal thought leads thee unto Eternity. Be brave! Be bold! Be as strong as adamant! Dost thou desire to realize God? Then, my boy, there is no time for *caring* for the body. Now is the time; even now is the opportunity. Thou art the child of Reality; thy nature is the True. Therefore, plunge into the Living Waters of the Life of the Soul. Be unafraid! Learn to rise superior either to the joys or the miseries of life! Remember thou art the Soul! Remember thou art the Self!

'Go down deep—deep. And thou shalt find that thou art strong. Go to the bottom of thy nature. There thou shalt find that thou art genuine in thy spiritual effort. What matter a few failings! Learn that fear and weakness are physical! They arise from the body—that nest of dreams; but thou in thy inner nature art free and fearless. Sing a song of strength, my son! Sing a song of strength!

3   33

Thou art the child of Immortality. Thy destination is Reality. What are those fleeting experiences of a day but phantoms in the Vast Mirage? Either deify life, or deny it. No matter how thou dost this—realize Divinity. Whether the method be positive or negative, it is all the same.'

And there arose in my soul a sense of peace. A great calm arose, and in its quiet the passive all-pervading power of Omnipotence suddenly revealed itself. This was a power that gave strength to my soul. And the Voice of the Guru was made audible in this state of consciousness, and I spoke, 'Beyond time, ay, within time, I am Eternity.' Whether embodied or disembodied, all is the Spirit. In the heart there is ever Oneness. In the heart there is ever Peace. Deep beneath the storm on the surface, deep beneath the waves of manifoldness and of strife and all the woe that comes of these, there is the Undercurrent of Reality.

'Tat Tvam Asi! Tat Tvam Asi!'

34

XI

The Voice of the Guru, speaking in the hours of meditation, sayeth:

'Behold! There is an inner as well as an outer world. There is a world of soul as well as a world of form. And, my son, if there are marvels and mysteries and vastness and beauty and great glory in the outer world, there are inestimable greatness and powers and incommunicable blessedness and peace and unshakable foundation of Reality in the inner world as well. O my son, the outer is only a semblance of this inner world. And in this inner world thy true nature doth abide. Here thou livest in Eternity while the outer world is of time alone. Here there is endless and unfathomable bliss, while in the outer world sensation is accompanied by pain as well as by pleasure. Here, too, is pain— but O what blessedness of pain, the ecstatic anguish of not having fully realized the Truth, and such pain is the pathway to more copious blessedness.

'Come, draw thy nature within this inner world. Come—come upon the wings of ardent love for me. Is there greater or closer union than

35

that between the Guru and disciple? O my son, O my son, Silence is the nature of Love—Inexpressibility. And deep within the deepest folds of silence there is God. Abandon all outer concerns. Whithersoever I go, do thou come! Whatsoever I become, do thou likewise become. O for the Holiness of God! Many are the shrines of the devotee's heart where thought, like incense, rises unto God. *Spiritualize* everything thou doest. See the Brahman, the Divinity in form as well as in the Formless. Than the Lord there is no greater good.

'In the inmost recesses of the inner world, into which one enters by the way of ardent love or ardent prayer, there are universes upon universes of the Divinity in Revelation. And God is always near. He is near not in a physical sense; He is near in a spiritual sense as the very Self within the self of thee. He is the very Substance of thy soul. He is the Knower of all thy thoughts and of the most hidden and most silent aspirations of thy heart. Give thyself up. Love for the sake of love; work for the work's own sake. Go into the chambers of the Silence; come into the Presence of Reality. The more thou goest inward the nearer dost thou come unto me. For I am the Dweller within the Innermost. I am the Magnet which draws out the revelation and glory of thy soul. I am Spirit! I am Spirit, untouched by thought or form. I am the Invulnerable and the Indestructible! I am the Atman! I am Paramatman! Lo! I am Brahman! I am Brahman!'

How wonderful are the words of the Guru! My soul cries out, 'O Blessed One, Thou Thyself art God. Thou Thyself art the Teaching which Thou dost teach, the very Spirit of the universe. Lo, Thou art all in all. Thy nature is the One, though Thy Maya sheds the glory of the manifold. Thine is the greater glory of the One. For spirit is One, Spirit is an Essence of which there are no parts or divisions. Spirit is the One Light seen through variously coloured lenses. O Guru, O my Guru, catch me up into that Life which is Thine. O Thou art Brahma, Thou art Vishnu, Thou art Sadashiva. Thou art Brahman, Para-Brahman.

'Hara Hara, Vyom Vyom,
Mahadeva!'

Thereupon my soul was caught up, as it were, into the Seventh Heaven, and I perceived the Divinity of Humanity, the great glory even of human weakness. I saw that everything was Divine; and within this Radiance stood the Guru as another Krishna transfigured upon a mount of realization in that inner world. Deep—deeper than time—more all-embracing even than space is that inner world of meditation. There can be no darkness, for all is effulgence. There, there can be no ignorance, for all is Jnana. There death cannot stalk, nor fire burn, nor water wet, nor the air dry. There is the region of the Ancient One, beyond all the lie of life; there is the Immovable Infinite.

And in that glory, speaking from the Innermost, the Guru spoke, 'My son, thine is the heritage. Infinite Strength is thine. Art thou then weak when thy power is the All-Power! Thou canst not rest satisfied with the show of sense. Death and Forgottenness are behind the pageant of the outer world. The body becomes the corpse when death has seized it. But the Spirit is ever free. It is the unembodied; It is the Witness—for though the bodies are destroyed, It can never be destroyed.' My soul, communing with the Guru, said, 'Then, O Lord, how wonderful! There is no death! There is no death!

And the Guru made answer, 'Ay, and neither life of sense, rooted in desire. For those that thirst for them is the mud-puddle of the world. Like oxen revelling in the mud, their bodies covered with mud, thus art those souls who revel in the foulness of lust. Long is the path for them, beset with Maya, the substance of the warp and woof of desire. Go thou beyond! Thy time shall come. Look up! Above are the Eternal Lights! Look up; and they *shall* penetrate the opaqueness of thy soul!'

Hearing these words my soul remembered—Divine is the nature of the Self, and Freedom is the Goal. And the Goal is Now and Here, and not Hereafter! And the destiny of the soul is certain—Self-realization, where time is blotted out, where the physical and mortal consciousness is dispersed, where the Light which is Life and the Truth which is Peace shine forth, where all dreams end, where desire is swallowed up in Infinite Realization—the Region of the Great Vast. O for the feeling of that Immensity! O for the blotting out of time! O for the destruction of the images of sense; O for the Freedom of the Infinite!

Hari Om Tat Sat!

XII

And the Voice that dwells in the Silence, speaking in the hours of meditation, said unto my soul:

'Come, my son, into the deep, deep Quiet. Beyond the tumult of personality, beyond its manifold experience, come into the Great Peace. Do not be troubled by the storm of passion or desire on the surface; do not be alarmed. Though the clouds gather thickest, beyond them the sun doth shine. In the Stillness the heart throbs best with quiet rapture. Make thyself open to the Love that is everywhere. How musical is the Stillness! What Peace it brings forth! O for the Infinite Stillness! O for the Infinite Peace!

'In all eternity not one good thought, not one spiritual longing is lost. Therefore go thou beyond the power of time; in that dost thou think great thoughts, and in that mayest thy soul desire the Infinite. In thine own mind doth thine own universe exist. And thou canst make eternity reveal even within the flux of time; by thy thoughts thou canst reach out beyond the bounds of space.

'O what power, what sense of exaltation,

what immeasurable sensing of Immensity come with the knowledge that the Self is free, that nothing can bind it! That thou comest or that thou goest, that thou dost do or that thou dost not do—what are these! They are but episodes within the great dream of life. They are but currents within the running stream of time—while the Self is the Eternal.

'Deep—deep—fathomlessly deep is the Silence; the Peace is immeasurable. Blot out all images of sense and thought. They are only refractions; go thou within the Light Itself.'

And the Voice added:

'O in the Self there is no sense of self; boundless, everlasting, absolutely free. It is the Unit knowing no diversity. In the Kingdom of the Self there is no room for thou, or I, or he. It is all That—the Om Tat Sat, incomparable and inexpressible. Who knows that Self, yea verily he *knows.*

'True love is that yearning to be free, to become merged in the Infinite. True love is that great yearning for the Silence. It will not be disturbed. It reaches out silently yet all-comprehensively. It is irresistible. It gains the Goal. Wherein all the gods merge, wherein all sound is lost, wherein form is swallowed up and thought

41

remains unthought, wherein life and death no more exist—know That to be the Self. Wherein struggle ceases, wherein Realization lies, wherein all that is relative is blotted out, wherein Beauty and Holiness, Sin and Terror, Good and Evil lose distinction, wherein the mind in contemplation becomes omniscient—know That to be the Self.

'My son, there is a Height beyond the greatest heights, there is Divinity beyond the greatest gods. There is the background of the Indestructible. All vanishes, all is blotted out—that which endures is the Self.'

And as the Voice became still it seemed as if my soul arose into the Vastness. Then 'I' was not. There was only the Light—the Light!

XIII

When the soul rose into the Stillness of the Innermost, the Voice made itself heard thus:

'Deeper than sin, deeper than evil is goodness. The fabric of the universe, its essential element, is goodness—infinite, incomparable goodness. There can be naught of evil where there is God. Evil is phenomenal and never real. Deep, deep in the sea of the soul are the immovable rocks of wisdom and of truth. Against these, all error and darkness and all evil must perish. True, on the surface there may be the violent noise of hurrying winds of desire, tempests of seething passion, hours of evil and of darkness, but Realization—one moment of Realization—is *Omnipotent*. It sweeps aside all manner of raging and rampant evil. It is like the effulgence of the sun, blasting all darkness. Therefore, even in the darkness, remember the Light; even in the very midst of thy sinning, call upon the Name of the Lord! And He, the Lord, shall hearken to thy prayers. He shall send His Angels to help thee. There is no power greater than the soul's own. Deep down is the flow of perpetual and unit Divinity. One

43

glimpse of That, and all sense of diversity in which sin and ignorance make their abode will disappear. In essence, thou art free, thou art pure, thou art divine. All the forces of the universe are at thy beck and call.

'Shalt thou struggle for freedom when thou art free! Thy aim must be the acquirement of spiritual knowledge. A single ray of the Flame of the Beatific Vision destroys and eradicates the subtlest shades of evil. Know that thou art of the Strength and the Effulgence of the Eternal! Thy life is neither here nor there! It is stationed in Eternity! All this sense of sin, in the deepest sense, is ignorance. It is a dream. The nature of sin is weakness; be thou strong! One glimpse of That which thou art—and thou art That, the Effulgent and Omnipotent!

Then heard I the Voice cry out, as though in prayer:

'O builder of these tabernacles of sense and thought, destroy that which thou hast erected! Encased in fear, sex, food, and sleep, and the thoughts that spring therefrom, thou hast, as it were, willingly enshrouded thyself in the denseness of ignorance, and thou goest on dreaming. Thy curse is thine own ignorance. Break down all dreams; destroy both the ideas of pleasure and

44

pain, and the iron bar of the body-consciousness will be flung aside. Therefore the task before there is prodigious. The web of Maya is as thin as the spider's, and yet equally as hard as adamant. O soul, come to thine own rescue! This tabernacle thou hast built; this tabernacle thou must destroy! And the process of such destruction is thine own Self-realization. This involves the divine awareness of the Oneness. Shall the sun and the stars and even space itself swallow up thy nature? The Soul is one-d with thee! Out of the darkness, out of ignorance, O soul! It is all self-imposed. Better pain than pleasure! Better misery than enjoyment! For these mould the forms of thought and sense into the shapes of fit vehicles for the revelation of the Spirit. Be thou the lover of the Terrible, O Soul! And though in the vision of the Terrible thou shalt behold Death—lo, verily, thou shalt also behold Immortality! Life is at best a dream. There is the Great Beyond. In the end unity is everywhere, a divine, all-embracing unity. It is all the same Sun, though its rays be manifold. And the ray is the Sun, and the Sun, the ray. And thou— thou art the Sun—the Sun! And even in the darkness there is Light.'

Hearing this, my soul passed into the deeper and yet deeper stages of meditation; and I knew, yea, verily, the ray itself as the Sun.

Again the Presence came in the hours of meditation, speaking:

'In the Silence, past all sound, in Eternal Peace thy nature dwells! Far from the tumultuous noise of sense, far from the agony and pain of life, far from the sense of sin and woe—and yet even in their midst, dwells the Divinity that IS. How wonderful the weaving of the dream! And yet, more wonderful is the Dreamer than the dream! Immortal, past the boundaries of death, stainless, even in the presence of enormous evils, art thou, O Soul—and rooted in Divinity. Good and ill— these are of the measurements of thought; and beyond thought art thou, the Effulgent and Supreme! The splendours of thy nature transcend all things! Incomparable art thou, beyond the terms of speech. O Effulgent and Celestial and Divine One, crowned in meditation's and Realization's height, who shall call thee sinner, or even saint; who can speak or even think of thee!

'O One in all, in all the same undying Self, who shall refer to thee in the terms of mortal life! Beyond art thou—Immortal. And, within even the turmoil of tempestuous thoughts, know there is the Silent Watcher of all things. His Light the will-o'-the-wisps of sense can never blind; nor can His

46

Peace be repressed by all the strife of life. Immovable, unthinkable is He, beyond the sun, beyond the moon and stars. He is the Self; the Self is He; He is the victor in the wars of the sense!

'However the mountain-heights of ignorance loom up, however the deeps of sin and woe be deep, He is the Encompasser of height and depth; He is the All, the One, the Engulfer of all variance! Know this and be thou Free, the Free!'

And the words came unto my soul:

'Lo, I am ever near. When the network of thy sin is drawn closest, and thou dost labour in utter darkness, know I am there suffering with thee the enormities of thy sin. I am conscious of thine inmost Self, knowing well the workings of thine inmost soul. Thou canst keep naught from me, who am ever present, not even a grain of thy secret thought. I am in thee; I know thee well. Without me thou canst not move nor breathe. Remember I am thy Self, going whither thou dost go, remaining where thou dost remain. Come, enfold thine heart in mine. Make it thy very own. Then all shall be well. Shadow and Silence—in them I dwell—within, in the tabernacle of thine heart. Go now! Go thou into the world and preach my word as wide as is the Self, for it is its life. My blessings thou ever hast, and all-embracing love!

47

Mine is as a mother's love for thee; as is a dove's love for its young, such is mine for thee. When trouble comes or danger threatens, remember I am thy servitor, the lover of thy soul!'

When these words had ended, I knew that the Guru had spoken, washing away all my sins, and I cried out:

'O ecstasy intense that my heart knows, being in the Presence of my Lord! One in Him, one in Him! How sweet the flow of such divinest thought!' And with the saints I exclaimed unto my self, 'Plunge into the Sea of the Lord. O fool, plunge into the Sea of the Lord!'

XIV

When my soul had entered the Silence of
meditation, the Voice of the Guru said:

'My son, do I not know all thy weaknesses?
Why dost thou worry? Is not life beset with trials
and tribulations? But thou art a Man. Let not faint-
heartedness take possession of thy soul. Remember that within thee is the Almighty Spirit. Thou
canst be what thou choosest. There is only one
obstacle—thyself. The body rebels, the mind
wavers—but of the end be sure. For nothing can
ultimately withstand the power of the Spirit. If
thou art sincere with thyself, if in the depth of thy
self there is integrity, then all is well. Nothing can
have full or final possession of thee. Cultivate
openness of mind and heart. Conceal nothing
from me with reference to thyself. Study thy mind
as though it were a thing apart from thee. Speak
frankly concerning thyself to those with whom thy
soul finds true association. For the gates of hell
itself cannot stand against a soul which is sincere.
Sincerity is the one thing needed.

'After all, most of thy faults arise out of the
body-consciousness. Treat thy body as though it

4

were a lump of clay. Make it subservient to the purposes of thy will. Character is everything, and the power of character is the power of will. This is the whole secret of the spiritual life; this is the whole meaning of religious effort. Behold the civilizations. How man glories over the pomp of sense-powers and sense-realities! But at bottom it is all sex and food. The mind of the majority has arisen out of these two all-comprising facts. We cover the corpse with flowers, but it is all the same a corpse. Therefore let the child of the Spirit be deep in his study of what the world calls great. For at heart it is all putrid, being grossly corporeal and physical. Have nothing to do with the ephemeral things of the world or with its attractions. Tear off the masks with which the body hides its shame. Enter into that insight where thou knowest that thou art not of these things. Thou art the Spirit; and know that the rise or fall of empires, the tendencies of cultures or of civilizations are of little import to the highest spiritual consciousness. Know That which is unseen to be truly great; know That to be truly desirable.

'Be thou the child of poverty; have thou an intense passion for purity. Lust and Gold make up the fabric of the worldly spirit. Root these out from thy nature. Know all tendencies thereunto to be poisons, one and all. Vomit out from thy nature all defilement. Wash thy soul clean from all impurities. See life as it is; and then shalt thou know it as Maya, neither good, nor yet evil, but something to be utterly given up, for it is all of the body and of the body-idea. Hearken to each whispering of thy higher nature. Seize avariciously each message of thy Self. For spiritual opportunity is a rare privilege, and unless thou takest heed, when the Voice enters the Silence, thou being busied with the call of the senses shalt not hear it; and thy personality shall fall into the clutches of habits that will cause it to perish. Only one message have I for thee; Remember that thou art the Spirit. The Power is behind thee. To be sincere is to be free. Be loyal to thy spiritual inheritance, for to be loyal is likewise to be free. Let every step which thou dost take be a step forward, and as thou goest along the highway of life, more and more shalt thou feel that thou art free. If thou hast integrity behind thee, thou canst face all men. Be true to thyself. Then shall thy words ring with the accents of reality. Thou shalt speak the language of Realization. And thou shalt gain the power which shall make others whole.

'Each man radiates the force of his character. One can never hide himself. If one is physically deformed, all men see the deformity. And if thou art spiritually deformed, likewise intuitively all men shall know. For when thou speakest of the things of the soul, men will feel that thou speakest that which is not in thy heart. Thou wilt not be able to communicate unto them anything whatsoever of the spiritual life. For thou thyself art not in and of it. Therefore if thou wouldst become a Prophet of the Most High, busy thyself with self-reform. Keep guard over thy nature; watch every impulse; spiritualize thy instincts. Be sincere. But I would charge thee to keep thy realizations in reserve. Cast not thy pearls before swine. If thou dost feel wondrous states of the Spirit, remain silent, lest by loud talk thou dost detract from their intensity. Ponder over what thou receivest. Go with all things into the silence of the Spirit. Guard all thy wisdom and all thy realizations as a thief guards his possessions. Thou must conserve thyself; and when thou hast practised silence for some time, then shall that with which thy heart has become full, overflow; and thou shalt become a treasure and a power unto men.

'There is one path of austerity which I recommend to thee. Meditate on the Terrible. For the Terrible is everywhere. Truly has it been said by a Sage. "Everything that one touches is pain."

Know this not in a morbid, but in a triumphant sense. In all mystical experience, in one form or another, thou shalt find this worship of the Terrible. In reality, it is NOT the worship of the Terrible. It is Terrible only to him who dwells in the senses. Pleasing and terrible are terms which have meaning only to one who is the bond-slave of the body-idea. But thou hast gone beyond—at least in thought and aspiration, if not in realization. By meditation on the Terrible thou shalt assuredly overcome the lust of the senses. Thou shalt embrace the life of the Soul. Thou shalt be made pure and free. And thus, more and more thou shalt become united with me who am on the other side of life. Never see life physically; study it psychically. Realize it spiritually. Then immediately the whole purport of the spiritual life shall be made clear to thee. Thou shalt know why saints love poverty and purity, and shun, by fight or flight, anything that savours of Lust and Gold.

'Let this suffice. Follow what I have said. Think over it until the nervous system takes it up, and the fever of these ideas and their loftiness and ecstasy course through thy veins, renew thy personality and make thee altogether whole.'

53

XV

When all was silence, in the deeps of meditation the Guru, appearing, said:

'My son, meditate on the Power which is the Mother's form, and then transcending all the fear the Power inspires, thou shalt go beyond the Power into the Mother's Spirit—which is Peace. Tremble not at the uncertainties of life. Though all the forms of the Terrible appear, multiplying themselves a thousandfold, remember, these can only affect the physical and not the spiritual self.

'Be steadfast and firm at all times, being fully aware that the Spirit is indestructible. Take thy stand on that which is the Self. Believe in nothing but that Reality which is innate alike in all. Then shalt thou remain undisturbed alike in the tempest or the seduction of appearances. That which comes and that which goes is not the Self. Identify thyself with the Self, not with the form. Impermanency predominates in the realm of things, in the objective world; permanency endures alone in that realm of eternal subjectivity wherein reigns the consciousness of the Spirit, free from the forms of thought and sense.

'That which is the True is immeasurable like the great ocean; nothing can bind or circumscribe it whatsoever. The predicates of existence do not apply to that shoreless Ocean of Divinity which rushes in upon the Self—as the Self—on the summits of Realization.

'The misery of the world is in direct ratio to desire. Have, therefore, no blind attachment. Bind thyself to nothing. Aspire to be; do not desire to possess. Shall any possession satisfy thy True Nature! Art thou to be bound down by THINGS! Naked thou comest into the world; naked thou goest forth when the summons comes! Wherein then shalt thou have false pride? Let thy possessions be those treasures that perish not. The increase of Insight is its own reward. The more thou dost perfect thy nature, the more readily dost thou acquire eternal possessions by which thou shalt, in time, purchase the Kingdom of the Self.

'Therefore, from this moment, go and grow inwards—not outwards. Invert the order of experience. Retreat from the sensuous life as lived for its own sake. Spiritualize everything. Make the body a tabernacle for the Soul; and let the Soul be more and more revealed day by day. Then shalt that darkness which is ignorance be gradually dispersed; and that light which is the Divine

Wisdom shall gradually be revealed. All the forces in the universe are behind thee, working in harmony for thy progress—if thou wilt but face Truth. As said the Lord Buddha, "The Tathagatas are only great preachers. You yourselves must make an effort". Ay, the Teachers can only impart wisdom; the pupil MUST assimilate, and this assimilation is the making of character; it is making wisdom one's own. By himself is one saved, by none other.

'Therefore, arise. Be diligent, and stop not till the goal is reached. That is the Command of the Upanishads!

'Even as a wild animal seeks for its prey, even as the slave of passion seeks for the gratification of his lust, even as a man dying from hunger desires food, even as the man who is being drowned calls for rescue—with that same intensity and strength of spirit do thou seek for truth. Even as a lion, not trembling at noises, even as a lion, fearless and free—so do thou roam about in this world, bent on the acquisition of Truth. For infinite strength is needed and infinite fearlessness. Go thou forth, knowing that all limitations shall burst asunder for thee, that for thee all crooked roads shall be made straight—if thou dost gather together the forces of thy Soul and if thou dost boldly tear off the MASK.

'Dost thou search for God. Then know—that when thou hast seen the Self, the Self shall be revealed to thee as God.'

'Om Tat Sat!'

And the Guru's Voice entered the Silence which is Peace—his Form that Radiance which is God!

XVI

Again the Voice made itself heard in the hours of meditation, saying:

'Peace be with thee, my son. Neither here nor hereafter is there any cause for fear. Interpenetrating all things is the great spirit of Love. And for that Love there is no other name but God. God is not far from thee. He is not bound down by the barriers of space, for He is the Formless One, reigning within. Resign thyself utterly to Him. Give Him all that which thou art, both good and evil—all. Let nothing be reserved. By such an act of resignation thy whole nature shall be made pure. Think how vast is the character of Love! It is greater than life and stronger than death; it is the quickest of all paths to God.

'Difficult is the path of Insight, easy the path of Love. Become thou as a child. Have faith and love. Then no harm shall befall thee. Be patient and hopeful. Then shalt thou be enabled readily to meet with all the circumstances of life. Be large-hearted. Root out all small-mindedness and thought of the small self. Surrender thyself with all trust unto Him. He knows all thy ways. Trust in His wisdom. How fatherly He is! Above all, how motherly is He! He is infinite in His long-suffering with thee. His mercy knows no bound. If thou doest sin for the thousandth time, lo, for the thousandth time and ever doth he forgive thee.

'Even should evil befall thee, it cannot be evil when thou lovest the Lord. Even the most fear-inspiring experience thou wilt recognize as a messenger from the Beloved. Through Love, verily, thou shalt attain God. Is not the mother at all times constant in affection? Even so is He, who is the Lover of thy soul. Believe, only believe—then all shall be well with thee. Do not fear what transgressions thou hast already committed. Be a man! Face life boldly! Let come what may, do thou remain strong. Remember that infinite strength is at thy beck and call. God Himself is with thee. What fear canst thou have?

'Make thy struggle for immortality here and now. Train the mind. That is the only important task. That is the great meaning and purpose in life. Now is the opportunity to demonstrate immortality by overcoming the body-consciouness, even when the Spirit is encased, as it were, in flesh. Do thou make thyself *worthy* of immortality. Even the gods worship him who has vanquished the body-idea. Death is only a physical event; long is the

59

life of the mind, and immeasurably long is the life of the Soul. How necessary, then, that thou shouldst think great thoughts, and thus hasten the course of thy spiritual evolution! Have done with things external. Even if a man master the whole universe, still has he to become the master of himself. Even if he discover all that is knowable, intellectually speaking, still he shall have to know himself. For Self-knowledge is the aim in life. Consciously or unconsciously, this is the aim which gives reason to life. It is this aim that explains the process of living, the process of Self-development. That knowledge is indeed worthy which leads to the improvement of the inner Self. Therefore set thyself bravely to the task of Self-knowledge. Long, perhaps, shall be the way, but there can be no doubt of the end. Leaving off all other words, be thou concerned with That which is the Highest!

'Stand on thine own feet! Defy the whole universe, if need be. What can ultimately harm thee? Be thou content with the Highest. Others seek for external riches. Seek thou the treasures of the within. The time shall come when thou shalt know that the empire of the whole world, ay, even the empire of the gods, is as dust before the splendours of Self-knowledge. Arise! Gird thy loins for the great effort! Come, great soul, thine is the heritage of the Divine Life. Thine are the riches of which no thief can rob thee. Thine are the riches of the Omnipotent Soul!'

XVII

The Voice, making itself heard in the stillness
of meditation, said:

'Terrible is the bondage of this world. Difficult is it to escape from out the net of Maya. Life
teaches us that in order to live truly one must go
beyond life, one must conquer death. This is the
supreme task, and the way to this conquest is
through the victory over those physical instincts
that lead unto death. I speak deeply to thee, my
son, asking thee to keep wide, wide awake and pay
heed to all that which comes to tempt thee. The
only way in which to progress spiritually is to anticipate the faintest rise of temptation. Keep strict
guard over thy mind. Constantly busy thyself with
that which is great and noble. In this manner thou
shalt gradually make thyself free.

'When temptation comes, it often comes, as
it were, of a sudden, before the mind has time to
become aware of what is happening. One is ap-
parently hurried on to the point of yielding. All
saints understand this. Therefore they anticipate
evil thought; defeating its strength and the possibility of its arising by strenuous good thought. By

thought is one made and unmade. Beware, then, that thou dost think good thoughts.

'Remember that it is the mind which thou must keep constantly buoyed up. Never let it be idle. Idleness is the counterpart of evil, the nest wherein it bears itself most fruitfully. Beware of idleness. Take life seriously. Realize the shortness of time and the greatness of the task of Self-unfoldment before thee. Now is thy time; now is thy opportunity. Bitterly shalt thou repent if thou dost allow thyself to drift carelessly into conditions of limitation and struggle, worse than those in which thou dost now find thyself. Be worthy of a better future, a better birth, by making thy present life a success of the spirit.

'The world abounds with death. The law of Karma is inevitable. Take heed, lest death find thee in the midst of thy sinning, and lest Karma follow thy yielding to physical desire with increased bondage and dire misery. My son, after thou hast once tasted of the nectar of immortality, how is it possible for thee to feed on the husks of swine?

'Yet, do not be alarmed. The Grace of God is greater than mountain-loads of sin. So long as thou dost believe, so long is there hope. But the way is almost infinite in length. Think of the lifetimes necessary for the complete eradication of evil, for the final transformation of the human into the divine consciousness. Canst thou, then, not understand how seriously thou shouldst labour for thine own good? And if thou dost love me, wilt thou not, for my sake at least, try to reach the Goal? How long have I waited for thee to be made whole and to struggle manfully! I have yearned for thy righteousness. I shall always stand by thee; I shall always love thee, but thou must shake off thy lethargy. Come out of thy moral slothfulness; come, be a man!

'Thy love for me is the pole-star of thy life. It is the basis of thy being. And there is good reason, for by thy love for me thou shalt be saved. Devotion to the Guru is the one thing needed. That will straighten out all thy difficulties. So be of good cheer. Know always that I am with thee. My longing for God, my Realization, all that I am or possess, shall be given unto thee, for it is the pleasure of the Guru to give even himself, if need be, for the good of the disciple. Once I have accepted thee, it is for ever, for eternity. Now, go in peace, and be mindful that if thou art true to thyself, thou dost add even unto my glory and even unto mine own vision.'

XVIII

The Voice of the Guru spoke unto my soul:
'My son, there is nothing so fascinating as the history of thine own development. It is the development of personality that makes life interesting. Be the witness! Stand aside, as it were, and observe thy personality as though it were a thing apart. Study the wayward thought, the fleeting desire. How transient the importance of yesterday's experience! What doth anything matter a decade of years hence! Thinking this, go through life undisturbed. Nothing which is earthly matters. It passes. Therefore give thy time up to things of the Spirit. Be unattached. Plunge into meditation. Let thine be the monastic spirit. The value of any experience or of any idea is its tendency in the way of making character. Realizing this, do thou acquire a new perspective in life.

How much time do the worldly give unto the body—that fragile bit of clay! How much are their minds concerned with ephemeral physical things! They perish in perishable things. They are swallowed up in Maya. Refrain, therefore, from concerning thyself with worldly things. Shun the society of the worldly-minded. How subtle is the mind! It endeavours constantly to idealize the physical. That is the witchery of Maya. Be not deceived by false beauty and by the gaudiness of appearances. Lose not thy insight. From immemorial time this struggle has been going on. What is all earthly attachment compared with the love of God for thy soul? Attachment is of the body, and therefore is bondage. But thou lovest me with thy soul. That is the difference. My son, it has not been amiss that thou shouldst pass through much pain in order to realize the danger and falseness of the world. The more thou dost suffer, the closer art thou brought to me.

'Cultivate passivity! Thou art altogether too irresponsible and too aggressive. Before thou seest the faults of others and dost criticize them without mercy, discover thine own glaring faults. If thou canst not bridle thy tongue, let it rant against thyself, not against others. First of all, keep thine own house in proper order. Such precepts as these are in direct accordance with the highest philosophy of Self-realization. For there can be no Self-realization without character. Humility, meekness, gentleness, forbearance, the non-seeing of evil in others—all these are the practical elements in Realization. Pay no attention to what others do to thee; be busied with thine own improvement. When thou hast learned this, thou hast mastered a great secret. Egotism is at the bottom of everything. Root out egotism. And as for passion, keep careful guard. Thou canst not be SURE of victory over it until thy body is laid at the burning ghat. Make thy mind the Smashana (funeral ground) and burn into ashes all thy desires if thou desirest to be free even in life.

'Thou must learn "blind" obedience. What art thou but a child! Hast thou any real knowledge? Be led along the path even as a child is led. Give thyself up entirely to my wishes. Am I not even as a mother unto thee in my love? And yet I am as a father unto thee as well, inasmuch as I do not spare the rod of chastisement. If thou wouldst be a Master, first of all learn how to be a disciple. Discipline is what thou requirest.

'Before, thy enthusiasm for my cause was boyish and effervescent. Now it is becoming tempered by true insight. The child is thoughtless, the youth is wilful; it is the man that is worth while. My intention is to make a man of thee in the spiritual sense. I would have thee deep, responsible, earnest, well-disciplined, and make manifest thy loyalty and love for me in steadfastness and sincerity of character. March forward. My love and blessings are ever with thee.'

67

XIX

In the hours of meditation I heard the Voice addressing me:

'Have no bitterness in thine heart. Be candid with thyself. Root out all false notions with regard to thyself. Root out all false attachment. See Divinity instead of body. See thyself as others see thee. Above all, have no false self-commiseration. Be strong! If thou must have faults, let them be the faults of a lion.

'The Law is mighty. It will crush thy heart and shatter thy personality in exact ratio to thy self-will. But it will also lead thee to true Self-knowledge. Base thy faith, therefore, on the Law. Action breeds reaction. Therefore let thy actions proceed from purity of heart and thought. Then shalt thou know Peace.

'Under the name of sentiment oftentimes a multitude of sins is covered: at bottom the grossest physical instincts may be at work. Throwing a cloth of gold over them does not mend matters. One is liable to idealize the purely physical sensations as lofty emotions. But discrimination tears off the disguise and teaches that false attachment

68

is always self-centred, dominating, cruel, and con-
scienceless. It is wilful, blind, and body-bound.
True love, on the contrary, is pure, related to the
Spirit, gives infinite freedom to the beloved one
and is full of wisdom and self-renunciation. Vomit
out from thy heart, accordingly, all attachment
and misplaced sentiment. And once you have
done it, as thou wouldst not as much as look at thy
vomit, being repelled, do not even as much as
think of attachment. It is bondage, terrible bondage. Remember this and march on bravely to
Freedom's Goal!

'Monasticism is the highest of all vocations.
By cutting thyself loose from all bondage, thou
dost help all that have known thee or shall ever
come into thy life. By self-realization the monk
fulfils all duties. By his self-sacrifice others are re-
deemed. Be thou a monk in thy heart and deeds.
Depend on nothing or on no one. Give others
their freedom and be thou thyself free.

'Be not disheartened because of thy disadvantages, for thy very disadvantages, given a
spiritual direction, shall be transfigured into ad-
vantages. Spiritualize thy feeling. Then, when no
malice or nervous irritation exists in thy nature,
thou shalt stand on thy ground, and yet be a light
and help unto many, though thou shouldst not

even see them. Be a lion; then all weakness will fall away from thee. Aspire to be a God; then the limitations of thy body-consciousness will disperse. Thou shalt become pure Spirit. Take thy lesson from the sublime phenomena of Nature—the mountains, the vast seas, and shining suns. Become one with strong things.

'Self-regeneration, my son, is a long and painful process. Before thou canst grow, it is necessary that thou be overwhelmingly frank with thyself. All veils of self-excuse or self-commiseration must be rent asunder by repeated experiences of pain and the limitation of thy pride. There can be no foolishness with God and no hypocrisy with thine own soul. The finest and best must come forth. Be grateful, therefore, for each messenger of pain, that reveals at once thy weakness and thy Self to thee. Exclaim, "Blessed, blessed pain!"

'A little learning has made thee an intellectual egotist; a greater learning will make thee spiritual. Remember that mind is not the soul. So let experience pound the mind as it will. It will purify it. That is the main thing. Gradually the Sun of the Soul will pierce the dark clouds of ignorance; and then the goal shall be revealed to thee, and thou shalt be merged in its effulgence.'

XX

Continuing his instructions, the Guru said:

'Inch by inch I shall master thy personality. Step by step thou shalt be forced nearer unto me. For I am thy Lord and God, and I shall not tolerate any idols of sense or sense-idealized thought between me and thee. Rend the veils, my son! Rend the veils!'

Then knew I that the Guru himself had become responsible for me. A great burden seemed to have fallen off from me. He continued:

'The mystical experience is good but better than the mystical experience is the consciousness that character brings. Character is everything; and character can come only through renunciation. Pain and affliction draw out the powers of the Soul and make character. Welcome them! See the Divine opportunities these create. "Diamond cuts diamond", as the saying goes, and pain alone conquers instinct. Blessed, blessed pain! The great devotee, Kunti, prayed that her lot might always be affliction, in order that thereby she might always remember the Lord. My son, hers was a true prayer. Do thou pray likewise. If thou lovest me,

71

know that pain will bring thee all the closer unto me, thy higher nature will shine forth.

'The mortal must be crushed out and crucified if the immortal is to be made manifest. The real "You" is behind the temporary configuration of consciousness. No insularity, my son! Thyself having adopted a certain course in the spiritual life, why become fanatic therein? God is not to be realized in one way, but in every way. Wheresoever there is glory or greatness, there the Lord Himself is manifest. Break down all walls! No special bounds are assigned to thee. Be all-sided; thy sole duty lies in self-perfection. Who commanded thee to preach any *one* idea to the exclusion of *all* others! Who commanded thee to preach at all? I have opened thine eyes to some extent. Before, thy vision was blurred. Now, thou art coming to know that before thou shalt teach others, thou must train thyself. Beware of conceit! Underlying so much of seeming selflessness and seeming aspiration to do work is this deep-rooted passion. Verily, egoism is the greatest curse. Harness thyself first! With thy mind running hither and thither, how canst thou hope to do good unto others? Concentration is the first thing needed. Thy surface consciousness is as wayward and as untutored as that of a rebellious child. What is wanted is that thou dost bring the depth of thee, the real man that thou art, to the surface. This being god at one moment and slave to passion at another, will never do! My boy, character, as I have said repeatedly, is the only test of Vision.

'The glamour of romance and idealism stands between today and the days of Buddha and the Rishis. The earth was then the same as now. The summer was hot, the winter cold, passion held sway in the hearts of men, and poverty and wealth, health and sickness were side by side. There were jungles and mountains and rivers, and cities and bazaars; and death then as now stalked everywhere. The same difficulties were to be contended with. Buddha looked upon the same world as thou thyself dost look upon. So the same realization is possible. Set thyself to the task! The Vedas themselves were expired in exactly as human an environment as thou seest today. Set thyself to the task, my boy!

'It is the conscious mind that must be taken in hand. This is the instrument which, when perfected, will enable thee to explore the hidden depths of the subconscious mind and to burn out old Samskaras (mental impressions and tendencies) which, now and then, rush up from beneath the threshold. And by this same conscious mind, spiritualized, the highest Super-consciousness may be attained. From the known, man proceeds to the Unknown. Knowledge is the conquest gained through the expansion of the conscious mind. More and more of the infinite territory of thought is acquired. The end is—Omniscience. True knowledge, my son, is not material, but spiritual. It is the *man* that is revealed through knowledge, not the *thing* !

'True knowledge is always a process of conscious realization. The assimilation of ideas, like the assimilation of food, touches and acts upon the conscious personality. The nervous system must assimilate ideas. Then the very body itself becomes full of *chaitanya*. The very body is made Spirit. It was in this sense that some of the Masters have said, "Even physically I am *chinmaya*!" That is why even physical service to the Guru is a privilege. The body itself then becomes Spirit in the process.

'One of the greatest tasks thou shalt master, my son, is Self-communion. Now thy concentration is largely dependent on circumstances and environment. Thou findest need to commune with others. But other minds may give thee only the stimulus. Thou thyself to thyself dost speak even when speaking to another. But knowledge, the true stimulus, should come from within. Why depend on another! Like a rhinoceros march on alone!

'Mind itself becomes the Guru, my child. This is an old teaching. And why? Because, pressing in upon the mind for Self-realization is the Divinity thou art. I and all others are only aspects of the Great Reality. The consciousness that I wore on thy plane, when in the body, was, as it were, only a window through which thou dost behold the Infinite. But the consciousness which was I, I myself make effort to merge in the Divine. What is Real in me, what is Real in thee, is that Brahman! Worship the Brahman, my boy. Worship that Brahman alone!'

75

XXI

Then quoth a Voice, speaking of the glory of the Guru unto my soul:

'Child, have unbounded faith in thy Guru. Through His mercy, through His illumination thy very inmost Soul has been resurrected. He has sought thee out, and through Him thou hast been made whole. The realization of the Guru descends in torrents upon the disciple. It is ceaseless; and nothing can resist it. His love for thee knows no bounds. To all lengths He shall go for thee. Never shall He desert thee. His very love is proof of His Divinity, and even His curse is blessing in disguise.

'The Realization of thy Guru is a thing, present and concrete before thee! Through the transfiguration of His Nature, thou dost verily perceive the Divine. There is no other path for thee. Give thyself over wholly and entirely to the Guru. What, at bottom, are even *all* the gods? He who has realized His Nature is the greatest Divinity. Man, seeing the great glory of Him who has realized the Self, perceives that Realization in manifold forms. The Guru is *more* than personal-

76

ity; through Him, all aspects of the Divine shine
forth. Is He not Shiva Himself! Of the Great Guru,
Shiva Himself is only an aspect. Meditate on thy
Guru as Shiva, as thy Ishta (Chosen Deity), and at
the supreme moment of Realization thou shalt
find the Nature which is the Guru merged in thy
Ishta. Before thee stands one, made Incarnate
Divinity through Self-Realization. What then shalt
thou have with abstract gods or theological con-
ceptions! Wheresoever thou shalt go, He shall
follow thee. Because, for the sake of helping man-
kind, He has renounced even Nirvana itself. In
this He is verily another Buddha. That He has realized His Nature makes His personality all the
more real, all the more powerful. Having attained
the Brahaman-Consciousness, He is empowered
with superhuman life and knowledge. All the gods
bow down to Him who has become Brahman.
Through the perspective of thy Guru-worship, see
all the Divinity that IS. Thus all shall be made one,
and the highest Advaita Consciousness shall be
gained. For the Guru shall be seen in larger and
ever larger perspectives, even according to the
enlargement of thine own Jnana and thy Bhakti.
Through the supreme expansion of personality,
the highest selflessness which is the Self is realized.
There, Guru, God, and thyself, ay, the whole uni-

verse, are made One. That is the Goal. See the Guru through the perspective of the Infinite. That is the highest Wisdom. Through Guru-bhakti thou walkest on the highest path.

'In one sense, the Divine Man is more real even than Pure Godhead. Thou canst only understand the Father through the son. Before even thou dost worship God, worship the God-man! Apart from the Brahaman-realized Consciousness of Man, where is there God? Guru-worship is the highest for the disciple, because through thy worship of the personality of the Guru, all sense even of personality shall ultimately be lost. Wider and wider become the horizons of the spiritual vision. First the physical presence is required, then comes the worship of the person of the Guru. The next step is the going even beyond the physical presence and the worship of the Guru, for the Guru teaches that the body is *not* the *soul*. Like a child has the disciple to be educated. From the physical to the·perception of the Guru's message and ideas; from the *person* to the *principle*. Mind and body cannot count in that supreme of all intimate relationships. The very Soul of the Guru is transmitted through lofty and still loftier realizations. More and more does the personality of the disciple merge in the Guru-Nature, while all the time the Guru's personality is seen to merge more and more into That of which even His *body* had been a manifestation. Then the sublimest Oneness is attained. The waters of the dual personalities of Guru and disciple become the Ocean of the Infinite Brahman! For the attainment of that Supreme Beatitude, wilt thou not go wheresoever He commands! For His sake, if He so wills, thou wilt gladly go through a thousand births and deaths. For thou art His loving servant; His will is thy Law. Thy will has become the instrument of His will. To follow Him—that is thy Dharma! For, as the Scriptures say, "Verily, the Guru is God, the Guru is Brahma, Vishnu and Mahadeva. He is indeed the Supreme Brahman! There is none higher than the Guru!'"

XXII

Then, in another hour of meditation, the Guru spoke:

'My son, at any moment the hour that brings death may come; make therefore the most of life. When a lofty inspiration visits thy soul, seize it avariciously, lest through thy sin of omission it is lost utterly. For every ideal sentiment, there is a practical realization. The method of realization is equally as important as the perception of the ideal itself. What is all grandiloquent talk compared with an ounce of practice? Talk may rouse emotion, but both time and feeling are wasted unless thou dost assume the responsibility the ideal demands of thee. Have no hypocrisy in thine heart. Throw not a cloth of gold over thy inaction and call it resignation. Behind all thy lack of response to spiritual stimuli, be sure there is always the physical consideration. If it should enter thy mind to take some daring course in the spiritual life, it is likely that thy body shall arise, asking, "Mind, shall it be comfortable?" Ah, for the sake of physical reason how far short hast thou fallen from the ideal!

'My son, courage is as much needed in the spiritual life as it is in the struggle which ensue in the world. As much perseverance as the miser has in hoarding gold, as great courage as the warrior has in rushing forth to meet the foe, so much perseverance, so great a courage must thou posses to accumulate the treasures that are imperishable and to master once for all the body and the body-consciousness. That is the secret that lies behind realization in any form—indomitable courage, courage that knows no fear. Develop the powers for self-analysis, then shalt thou find that when thou dost fail to take up boldly the life of true renunciation, it is because of the promptings of thy body which seeks to satisfy the narrow and selfish desires of the mortal self.

'But this body must be rooted out. It must go in some definite resolve to realize one's self as Spirit. Boy, take one plunge into the dark, and thou shalt find the very darkness hath become the light. Cut off all bonds, or rather subordinate the body to the greatest bond, that of the morrow's uncertainty, and immediately thou shalt find that thou hast gained the highest freedom and that the body itself will become the servitor of the Soul.

'Bold steps are needed in the life spiritual as in the life temporal. He who risks not can never

6   81

hope to gain. Throw the body overboard into the sea of uncertainty; be like the wandering monk, attached neither to person, place, nor things, and though thou lose the body, thou shalt gain the Soul. Boldness is the one thing needed, the boldness of a tiger in the jungle. Only strong hands can rend the veils of Maya. Speculation will never do; manliness is what is wanted. So long as there is fear for the body, so long there can be no realization for the soul. Think of the sacrifices made by the worldly in worldly pursuits. Wilt thou not make sacrifice in the spiritual pursuit? Is God to be realized by eloquence or by mere form! Get out from under all sheltering influences. Come out into the open. Make the Infinite the horizon. Let the whole universe be the field in which thou dost wander!

'Thou must welcome all experience! Come out of thy narrow grooves! Fearlessness will make thee free. As it is certain that in life Dharma *alone* is true, so it is equally certain that Sannyasa is *alone* the true spiritual path. Renunciation like religion is not a *form*; it is all-inclusive; it is a condition of consciousness, a state of personality. In realization thou thyself must come face to face with God; in renunciation thou thyself must find the peace eternal. No one can realize for thee; for thee, likewise, no one can renounce. Therefore, be brave and stand on thine own feet. Who can help thee save that which is the Self in thee? Making thine own mind thy Guru, thine own Inner Self thy God, march forth fearless as a rhinoceros. Let whatever experience come to thee, know that what is affected is the body, not the Soul. Have such faith and firmness that nothing can overpower thee. Then having renounced everything, thou shalt find that all things are at thy command, and that thou art no longer their slave. Beware of false enthusiasm, however. Care nothing either for pleasant or unpleasant sensation. Simply go forth, without a path, without fear, without regret. Be thou the true Sannyasin. Do not shelter thyself under false notions. Tear all veils asunder; destroy all bounds; overcome all fear, and realize the Self.

'Do not delay. Time is short and life is fleeting. Yesterday is gone; today is flying fast; tomorrow is already at hand. Depend on God alone! By renouncing thou obtainest all; by renouncing thou fulfillest all obligations; by giving up thy life thou dost gain Eternal Life. For, what life dost thou renounce?—the life of the senses and sense-fed thought. Go down into the deeps of thy personality! There thou shalt see that already a mighty undertow of the spirit is at work which shall some time soon lash the indifferent surface into a very tempest of renunciation and God-vision. Believe in they Self! Long enough has thou been indifferent. Now be sincere! Be tremendously sincere! Then all good things of the Soul shall be thine.'

XXIII

Again the Guru spoke:

'Already the word has been spoken; the commands have already been given thee. Now action is required. Teaching without practice is of no avail. How great would be thy sorrow that thou didst not put resolution and insight into practice long ago! Having gained the path, march bravely on. What shall stand in the way of one who has determined on Self-realization! When thou standest alone, God shall be thy companion, thy friend, thy all in all! Is it not better to forsake all in order that the Presence of God shall be felt all the more? When thou dost renounce Nature, Nature herself shall reveal her true beauty to thee. Thus to thee everything shall become spiritual. Even a blade of grass shall speak to thee of the Spirit.

'When thou hast renounced all and dost walk on lonely paths, remember that my love and wisdom shall be with thee always. Thou shalt be close, very close unto me. Thou shalt gain further insight, increased purpose of will, and a great increase of the universal sense. Thou wilt become one with all things. Renunciation, my boy, is the one path. Imagine thyself dead today.

'However it may rebel, know that some time, somehow the body must be sacrificed as a holocaust unto the Soul; the body-idea must be overcome. Thou canst make the long path, pursued by the lukewarm in spirit, short if thou art sufficiently sincere. Take time by the forelock. Take instant advantage of opportunity. If by one leap thou canst cross over the intervening barrier between thyself as thou art and thyself as thou shouldst become, hasten to do so. Turn on thyself like a tiger on its prey. Have no mercy on thy mortal self. Then shall the Immortal Self in thee shine forth.

'Pay no attention to trivialities, my son. What can details matter when the Universal itself has dawned upon thee? Details are purely physical. Centre not thy mind upon them. Be concerned with the One and not the many. Having the spirit of Vairagya, care not what details of experience may come to thee. Remember that thou thyself art thine own enemy as also thine own well-wisher. With one stroke thou canst cut off the bondage of a veritable host of past Samskaras. The necessary spirit once aroused in thee, the task will be an easy one. And my grace and blessings shall be with thee in the making and the strengthening of that spirit. Trust, and it shall be well with thee.

'Why concern thyself as to the opinion of others? What can such an attitude of mind avail thee? So long as thou lookest for the regard of others, so long thou mayest be sure that conceit doth still hold the citadel of thine heart. Be righteous in thine own eyes; then others may say what they will, thou shalt take no heed. Seek no advice; follow thine own higher inclination. Only experience can teach thee. Waste not thy time in idle speech. It will avail thee nothing. Each is guided by his own experience; therefore who can advise another? Depend on thyself in all ways. Look to thyself for guidance, not to another.

Thy sincerity will make thee steadfast; thy steadfastness will bring thee to the goal. Thy sincerity will also make thee resolute; and thy resolutions will make thee overcome all fear. My Blessings upon thee! My blessings upon thee for ever!'

XXIV

And the Voice of the Guru said:

'My son, draw thyself within the Innermost! Outward things are like darts and arrows that do but bruise the soul. Make thine Inner Self thy true abode. The great Magi Solomon hath said, "Vanity of vanities, all is vanity!" Ah indeed so! What is even the treasure of the whole world at the moment of death! How well also did Nachiketas of Upanishadic fame know! He conquered Yama himself through that great victory which renunciation brings. All that which possesses form must suffer death—the fate of all form. Even the mind itself is a form. It, too, is subject to change and to disintegration. Go thou, therefore, beyond both mind and form.

'From the highest standpoint nothing matters. In the supreme sense, once thou hast given thine heart to thy Lord, nothing can bind thee. This should give thee a wonderful sense of freedom and expansion. This should make thee fearless. Love is the greatest power. By the power of love all veils which blind thy vision of the Beloved One can easily be rent asunder.

'Purify the mind! Purify the mind! That, once and for all, is the whole and only meaning of religion. Develop continuity of thought along the highest line. More and more develop consistency of purpose. Then nothing can withstand thee. Thou shalt move unto thy goal as readily as the eagle flies. O that one could think at all times of the Highest! That in itself would be Freedom.

'Rouse thyself from thy sluggishness. Reconstruct thy whole nature. Open thine eyes to the beauty which is everywhere. Commune with Nature. She shall teach thee many lessons, now unknown to thee. She shall bring to thee great calm of personality. See the Invisible Divinity even in the visible universe about thee. Be the witness! The actor is burdened with the effects of action; if thou must act, even in action be thou the witness. Concern thyself with nothing but Self-realization and self-analysis. Strengthen that which in thee is best. Pay no attention to the opinions of others. Be strong! Make thy very own self thy Guru. Saturate it to such an extent with great purposes and ideas, that of itself it shall seek and express the highest. Once strengthened, it shall arouse itself, and things undreamed of shall be revealed to thee.

'Refrain from criticism! Art thou thy

brother's keeper! Art thou the custodian of his actions! Who has placed thee as a judge above him! Blot out the slightest memory of another's evil conduct. Be thou concerned with thyself. Thou shalt find enough in thee to condemn and criticize. And yet thou shalt also find enough to give thee joy. For each unto himself should be his own universe. Let the human in thee die, so that the Divine shall be revealed. Is it not better to be at peace? Disturb thyself about nothing? Trust not in man, but in God! He will lead and guide thee.

'Stand like a rock in this Samsara, the sea of unrest. Walk through this interminable jungle of the manifold like a lion. Omnipotence is behind thee; but first crush out all desire for earthly or purely physical power. With the sword of discrimination cut in twain all that comes of Maya within thy path. Dictate to none; let none dictate to thee! Be unafraid of death, for if it should overtake thee even at this moment, know that thou art already on the Path and walk on fearlessly. Death is only an incident in a larger life. Even beyond death the possibilities and opportunities for spiritual progress exist. There is no end to what one may become. Everything depends on individual effort, and the Mercy of God is always at hand.

'Study everything about thee; and thou shalt

find that for thee in everything there is a spiritual message. The One reigns supreme, the One that is in every aspect of the Many. Worship the Omnipresent Unity even when the Manifold, by its distracting variety, would give the lie thereto. Appearances deceive, as the proverb says, but it is man's duty to detect this deception and see Reality behind all appearances. Each is the custodian of his own Karma; each is the breaker of his own bondage; each must for himself discover Reality. There is no other way. Each stands on his own ground; each must fight his own battles; and Realization is always a wholly individual experience. Ultimately, each is his own Saviour and his own Lord. For the Divinity-That-Is shall shine as the Unit Whole through each and every fragment of personality. Such is the teaching. That is to be realized. And that realized, the Great Goal will have been attained.'

XXV

Again the Voice of the Guru spoke unto my soul;

'Treat thy body as though it were a thing apart from thee. If thou shalt say unto it, "Do this," that it shall do. The Master has said, "Imagine thyself seated as a clock upon the mantelpiece and study thy daily comings and thy goings. Thou shalt find how vain and useless most of them are." Therefore cease placing any undue importance or attachment upon the incident of the hour. Ignore the physical, if thou canst not spiritualize it. To bring Divinity even into commonplace daily life is difficult indeed; but that is the test. It is not only upon the Heights, but in the valleys as well, that we must come face to face with God. How truly concentrated that mind that can gather glimpses of the Spirit even from the most ordinary circumstances!

'Root out the slightest trace of egotism. The more thou dost study thy personality, the more shalt thou find that egotism rushes forth in almost every experience, whether of action or of thought. Egotism is not only to be overcome, but verily to be entirely crushed out. Even in self-blame or self-pity this cursed phenomenon is seen to exist. The true man of Realization blames neither others nor himself. He ignores circumstances, being covered with mightier things.

'See thyself as already dead. Even in life separate thyself from the body. See the spirit, not the form of things. Then, in thy new and clearer vision the whole of life shall be seen in a new light and be made manifest to thee in new and loftier and altogether spiritual forms.

'Reflect much on the immense continuity of mental and moral experience. That man is born and reborn until progress has become merged in perfection, will then become self-evident. Each is creating, through thought, desire, and action, a world of which he himself should be the governor. It is not one, but innumerable bodies which the soul creates in its effort to sound the very bottom of the ocean of objective experience and pass beyond such experience into the full and subjective consciousness of Pure Spirit.

'Kill out any hankering for the occult and merely speculative. The increase of false knowledge or the acquisition of so-called psychic powers, in and for themselves, is pernicious as it intensifies the ego and makes for added selfishness.

The extension of consciousness in various ways in the spiritual process is an acknowledged phenomenon, and strictly incidental. When this, however, is placed superior to the aim of Self-realization, the process on the Path is hampered a myriadfold. Beware of the ego as thou wouldest beware of a mad dog. As thou wouldest not touch poison or play with a poisonous snake, even so keep aloof from psychic powers and those who pretend to these. Let all the faculties of thy mind and heart be directed to the Lord. What else shall be the aim in the spiritual life!

'Be independent! By all means, be independent! Place thy trust in thine own possibilities and the mercy of the Supreme. Faith in others will only make thee more and more helpless and miserable. If thou dost not believe in thyself, the most painful experiences will force thee to do so. The Law knows nothing of sentiment or self-commiseration. It shall grind thy animal nature into spiritual shape. It has but one aim, that of transforming thy character! Why tarry, then? Why put off until another life that which may be realized this very moment? Be sincere! Be tremendously sincere! Worthiness or unworthiness is not the question. Thy salvation is *assured*; for thou shalt be *forced* into the higher life. That is the destiny of each individual. Divinity *must* be made manifest.

'A glorious spiritual indifference is likewise necessary. Why take notice of the thousand and one irritating details the day may bring forth? Be thou free; realize that all these are only the currents of that mighty flow of past Samskara from which thou must for ever sever thyself. Let come what may; let concerning thee be said what may. To thee all these things must become as unsubstantial as a mirage. If thou hast really renounced the world, how canst thou be troubled any longer! Be consistent in effort as well as in idea and ideal.

'In the galleries of art, the critic studies various paintings, some ghastly tragic, some radiantly beautiful, but he himself is not actually affected by the emotions portrayed. Do thou similarly. Life is an art-gallery; experiences are, as it were, so many paintings hung upon the walls of time. Study them, if thou dost choose to do so; but free thyself from any emotional interest. Study, but be unaffected. Bearing this in mind thou shalt become, in very truth, the witness. Study thy mind and all thy experiences as a physician might study the body or its diseases. Be unsparing in thy criticism of thyself. Then shalt thou truly progress.

'The way is long. The process of education necessitates repeated lives. But one may live intensively and thus avoid the circuitous paths which are trodden by such as live extensively and only on the surface of their personality. Thinking deeply and continuously on spiritual subjects, and moulding desire into aspiration and passion into spiritual fervour—these are among the ways and means. Determine to be consistent each hour of the day until thy whole nature becomes charged with the spiritual idea and intention. Be always on the guard. Resign everything to Him who is the Dispenser of all good things. Embrace whatever will keep thee steady on the spiritual path, even though it be the fear of death. Thou art the young plant that needs support; catch hold of anything that makes thee strong. Cling unto it with might and main. Be steady, sincere, earnest-minded, righteous, and avail thyself of each moment and opportunity. Long is the way; time is flying. Therefore, as I have counselled repeatedly, set thyself to the task, devoting thy whole soul to it, and thou shalt reach the Goal!'

XXVI

The Voice of the Guru spoke:

'My son, thou wilt be compelled to learn that in this world there are certain difficulties with which thou must meet and which, because of thy past Karmas, will appear for thee insurmountable. Do not fret and fume over them. Know that wherever there are worry and expectations in work, there is also the blindest form of attachment. Having done thy task stand aside! Let the work's own Karma float it as it will down the stream of time. After having completed thy task let thy motto be "Hands off!" Work to thine utmost, and then to thine utmost be resigned. At all events, never be discouraged, for the fruits of work, be they good or ill, are all secondary considerations. Give them up and remember full well that in work it is not so much the perfection of work as the perfection of personality through work which should be the goal.

'Over thine own actions thou canst have sway; over the actions of another thou hast no power. His Karma is one, thine another. Do not criticize; do not hope; do not fear! All shall be well.

7

Experience comes and goes, be thou not disconcerted. Thou standest on sure ground. Let experience teach thee to be free, no matter what comes, do thou never forge any more bondage. And art thou so foolish as to be bound down by *one* form of work? Is not the scope of my work infinite? Do not debase the great ideals of Karma-Yoga and true work by jealousy and attachment! Let not childish emotions have hold over thee!

'Do not expect; do not anticipate. Let Samskara float thy personality whithersoever its currents may lead. Remember that thy true Nature is the Ocean, and be unconcerned. Know the mind to be the body in a subtle form. Therefore make thy austerity a mental one. Regard all thy moods as mere body-moods; remain aloof; thou art the Soul. Be concerned only with thy Self; lead thou thine own life. Be true to thyself.

'My son, take life calmly. At all times be at peace. Agitate thyself over nothing. Thy physical nature is too nervously Rajasika (active). But lose not thy Rajas; spiritualize it; that is the secret. Have thyself so well under control that at any moment thou canst quiet thy active nature and remain altogether in the meditative state. Be all-sided! Let thy relations with those with whom Karma brings thee into contact be such that thou dost bear

witness to the greatness that is within them. And
if thou must see faults, see first the beam in thine
own eye rather than the mote in thy brother's eye.
Be not overwhelmed by the experience of the
hour. Ten days hence what doth it matter!

'The whole meaning of the religious life is
to get rid of Ahamkara or egoism. So deep-rooted
is it that, like the cause of a deep-seated disease, it
is most difficult to discover. It disguises itself under myriad forms; but of all its disguises none is
so treacherous and so evil as the spiritual disguise.
Believing carelessly that thou dost work for spiritual purposes, thou shalt find that at bottom it may
often be selfish motives that do influence thee.
Therefore keep thou a sharp look-out. It is only
by the conquest and utter extinction of personality that the Sublime Impersonal can be understood and realized. To die to one's self in order
that one may truly live, that is the aim of the life
spiritual. Satisfied with will-o'-the-wisps, many fail
to see the sun. Real immortality can be gained
only when selfish personality is completely destroyed. Remember that! Fix the mind on the
Impersonal! It is the Light of the Most High that
shines through a self-conquered personality.
When that Light shines fullest, then the Effulgence of Nirvana is made manifest.

XXVII

In the silence of the hour of meditation, the Voice of the Guru spoke unto my soul these blissful words:

'My son, so long as there are ideas, so long will the form-aspects of idea persist. For this reason the gods and all spiritual realities are true essentially. The spheres of the universe are innumerable. But in and through them all shines the splendour of Brahman. When thou dost realize Brahman, then for thee, all planes and spheres and conditions of consciousness are made one. Therefore, accept all truths and worship all aspects of Divinity. Be catholic and universal. Widen the scope of religion, see the religious spirit as a possibility in all the walks of life. Wheresoever experience—whatever be its character—be interpreted spiritually, there the Voice of the Lord may be heard. Learn to see the other side in all matters. Then shalt thou never become a fanatic. Through the spiritual consecration even the most menial acts may become divine. See the whole universe as permeated with the Divine Life. Eradicate all sense of distinction; destroy all narrowness of vision; widen the perspective until it becomes infinite and all-inclusive. "Wheresoever there is righteousness," saith the Lord, "know that there I am manifest." The hedge around the young tree is useful; but the sapling must become the widespreading banyan, giving shelter and protection to all that comes within its shadow. Similarly, the sense of distinction may be useful for the growth of special ideas, but the time must come when the particular idea assumes a universal aspect. Be broad, my son, be broad. Make it an *instinct* to be broadminded. For what is to be achieved intellectually must be achieved emotionally as well.

'Regard the whole universe with equal love; through loyalty in thy individual friendship, come to understand that in each individualized life shines, potentially, that same beautiful Light thou dost behold in him whom thou hast called by the sweet name of "brother". Be universal! Love even thine enemy. These distinctions between friend and foe are only phenomena of the surface. Deep, deep, below it is all Brahman. Learn to see the Divine in everything and everyone; and yet be sufficiently guarded so as to avoid the unpleasantness and clash of temperament. In the highest sense the truest relationship is that which is relationless, and therefore spiritual. Learn to recognize the Universal instead of the particular, the Soul instead of the physical personality. Then to thy friend thou shalt be bound closer; even death shall not separate ye, and having overcome all distinction, in thine own self there shall be, also, no awareness of an enemy. See that which is beautiful in every form, but worship instead of craving to possess. Let every soul and form have a spiritual message for thee.

'All ideas are relative to the temperament from which they proceed; therefore, in listening to another, see the realization-side instead of the logic of his speech; then no argument shall ensue and thine own realization shall receive new impulses. Then know, also, that silence is oftentimes golden and that to speak and argue is to dissipate thy forces; and remember never to cast thy pearls before swine. All emotions are likewise relative to temperament; therefore be the witness, instead of being the attached one. Know that both thinking and feeling are in Maya. But Maya itself must be spiritualized; let thy self be Self-possessed therefore, and remain unattached. For what thou mayest think and feel today may not move thee on the morrow. And above all, know that, in thy real nature, thou art independent of both idea and emotion. These only help to reveal that which is truly thy Self; therefore let thy thoughts and feelings be great, universal, and above all selfishness. Then, even in this dense darkness of the Samsara, thou shalt see—though it may be at first but dimly—the Everlasting Light.'

XXVIII

The Guru spoke:

'Make no plans; it is only the worldly-minded that plan. Be independent of circumstance; make uncertainty thy certainty and live in strict accordance with thy Sannyasin's vows. Why pay any heed to what the morrow may bring? Live the present as thou dost find it and in the noblest way. Associate the name of thy Beloved One with each single circumstance of thy past, present, or future experiences. Thus they will be spiritualized. Regard them as thou wouldst study paintings on the wall. The subjects they represent may be tragic, commonplace or fascinating; be thou only the critic. Be they good or evil, know that the Self in thee doth stand apart from all experiences.

'And as for organizations, appreciate their usefulness, the greatness of the ideas they embody, but remain thou unidentified. The religious life is purely personal and subjective. It may be born in a church, but it must outlive it. Through law beyond law is the path of Realization. Know that and be free. Carry on work as it doth come to thee and be independent therein. If there must be organization, let it be the organization of ideas; but never labour for the extension of a purely organized form. No organization can save thee; thou must save thyself. Generally speaking, organizations, however spiritual and unsectarian their intent, degenerate into worldliness. Beware of any *churchianity*. Keep aloof from any dogmatism and fanaticism. Be all-inclusive.

'Be always true and loyal to the source from which thou hast received thy inspiration. Have faith and love; have hope and be patient. All these veils of illusion shall be soon rent asunder for thee, and thou shalt behold me, thy Beloved One, in my true nature. Be not bound down by my personality, or rather thy notion of it. I am not that which was in earth-life associated, like thine own personality, with limitation and human weakness. That personality I *assumed*; my real nature is That which *inspired* my teaching there. Know me as I am, not as I was. Know me subjectively as thy Self, and then thou shalt see the Self in all; then all sense of limitations and manifoldness will have no power over thee. I *am not external* ; I dwell within the Innermost. I live in thy thought; I am with thee in thy aspiration. Space and time relations have no power over the Soul, and cannot stand in the way of spiritual communion. I am thy Antaryamin

(Inner Ruler). Know me as such; and whether thou art born a myriad years apart from me, whether even at death the separating veils are not destroyed, that matters not. In Love and in Realization there are no barriers. I may even have *need* that thou shouldst labour and exist phenomenally apart from me; but I see through the veils even though thou dost not. I am present eternally with thee, whether thou art aware or not. The time shall come, however, when thou shalt be made aware. The tusks of the elephant having gone outward, never turn inwards; even so the love and insight of the Guru, having been once bestowed, have been bestowed for ever.

'By having become my servant thou hast freed thyself. Thy liberation is in very ratio to thy service unto me. And know that though thou dost labour for me, more precious in mine eyes than thy labour in my cause is the love and fidelity thou dost bear for me. The universe is infinite and time is eternal, but I am always at thy beck and call.

'Thou standest in need of no forms; it is the monastic spirit, not the monastic garb, that is of importance, and the true Sannyasa is the Vidvat-Sannyasa—the Sannyasa which is conterminous with illumined Insight. Let thy name be that of one striving for the goal. There is infinite development in the monastic life. The form is nothing; the life is everything.

'Be like Indra in thy strength. Be like the Himalayas in thy steadfastness. Above all, be self-less, and hold communion with thy self. Let thy Mantra be my Name. Let thy Yoga be the union of thy soul with mine, thy Realization be the conscious knowledge, that in the heart of things I and thou are ever One. Distinction is death; Sameness is Life.

'Thou hast heard my Voice; thou hast received my teaching; now obey implicitly; love infinitely; work selflessly. Be thou my instrument; let thy very *personality* be mine. Say, "Shivoham! Shivoham!" "I am He! I am He!"

'This whole universe is Brahman; That which is alike the Brahman in thee and in me—seek that Brahman, realize that Brahman in thy-self and in all as the One Absolute Existence, Knowledge, and Bliss—and be free, be free!'

XXIX

Hearing these words of the Guru in the hours of meditation day by day, I was made conscious of the real relation between the Guru and disciple. An immovable, eternal Realization hath become mine; and in life or in death, near or apart, I know that a Great, Living Presence is always nigh, a Presence that is unconfined by Time or Space, a Presence that can know no separation. And to the Guru I cried out, the while a Great Light surrounded me:

'Thou hast raised me up from darkness by Thy Grace. Thou hast taken me as I was—a mere nothingness—and hast made me what I am—a devotee who is conscious of infinite strength within him. From long since have I heard Thy Voice, and I listened as one intoxicated by some overwhelming music—some music previously unheard. But my own response was noisy and effervescent; and I understood not that which I had heard. Before, the Light on Thy countenance was too august, and I did not behold Thee as Thou art. Thus ignorantly and wantonly I did waste the treasures Thou didst so freely bestow; and lo, I have sinned as the vilest sinner even in Thy very Presence, inflicted my iniquities upon the very Love and Blessings Thou didst show unto me. I was most unworthy of Thee. In my conceit, I forgot Thee and did place myself on the pedestal of a leader of men, so that people might say of me, "Lo, he is great!" But now, O Lord, I have come to understand. With impure hands I defiled Thy teaching and desecrated Thy Presence. But Thy Mercies have been infinite; and Thy Love for me hath been inexpressible. Verily, Thine is the Divine Nature. Even greater than a mother's love for her own child, is Thy love for Thy disciple. O Lord, Thou hast scourged me with Thy Power until I am made whole, and moulded me as the potter moulds his clay into whatsoever shape he desires. Thy Mercy, Thy Patience, Thy Sweetness are Infinite. I adore Thee! I adore Thee! I adore Thee! Let my hands, feet, tongue, eyes, ears—my entire body, let my mind, will, emotions—my whole personality, be offered as a holocaust and purified in the flames of my Devotion unto Thee. My good, my evil—all that which I was, am, or shall be ever, life upon repeated life—I consecrate to Thee. Thou alone art my God and Salvation! Thou art my own Higher Self! Let me possess nothing; let me have no other home than Thy

Heart. Let my life be a radiance of purity now and for ever.

'Hari Om Tat Sat!'

XXX

And ever afterwards in the hours of meditation I felt a Living Presence within and about me; and filled with ecstasy I heard and repeated the great Mantra:

'Om! Thy very Self am I ever and ever!

'Thine is the Strength Infinite!

'Arise! Awake and stop not till the Goal is reached!

'Thou art Brahman! Thou art Brahman'

Om! Om! Om!

BOOKS ON SPIRITUAL LIFE

For a detailed publication list please write to:

Advaita Ashrama
(Publication Department)
5 Dehi Entally Road
Kolkata 700 014